CLIMBING UP THE MOUNTAIN

CLIMBING UP THE MOUNTAIN

By

Rev. Dr. Marcia E. Neveu M.Div.

Second edition revised 2013

Copyright © 2013 Rev. Dr. Marcia Elaine Neveu, M.Div.
Birmingham, UK
ISBN 978-1-905028-53-5
www.marcianeveu.co.uk
marcia@cccreatives.com
Edited, designed and published by Capital Cube Creatives
Published in 2013 by Capital Cube Creatives Birmingham, UK

All scripture is taken from the King James Version of the Bible unless otherwise stated.

iv

DEDICATION

This booklet is dedicated to my family, friends and colleagues who have been instrumental in my faith walk. Some have encouraged me to climb the mountain and some have climbed the mountain with me.

Husband – Alain

Parents – Elder Basgo and Muriel Lewis

Children - Maureen, Dwayne, Jean-Paul and George

and

Bishop Lloyd Henry

Rev John & Mrs Joanne Grey

David & Carol Howell

Raymond Harris

Sue Blyden

Gwen Daley JP

Lucille Elson

Adelaide Folkes

Paul Spence

and many others ....

TABLE OF CONTENTS

INTRODUCTION

Climbing up the mountain was written to encourage and remind you, the reader that God still speaks through every circumstance of life that you face. It is also to remind you, that God is still alive; that He still works miracles and that you can call on Him at any time and in every situation.

My prayer is that whatever situation you face in your life, you will recognize the opportunities that God has orchestrated and make the most of them. In all that we go through, there is a lesson to be learnt and with the help of Jesus Christ we can always be victorious.

Let the life that you live, be a reflection of the New Man inside. Therefore if any man be in Christ, he is a new creature: old things are passed away; behold, all things are become new. (2 Corinthians 5:17)

Have you ever wondered if God still speaks to His people today? And if so, how does He speak to His people? Then, in asking these two questions, you might also have to consider if you were to hear God speaking what would be your response to His voice? The testimonies of victory that follow, (which are only a small selection of many), were made possible because I responded to the call of God and trusted Him for what often seemed an impossibility.

My desire is that everyone comes to the realization that the call of God is unique to each individual and that nothing is impossible when it is placed in the hands of God.

Throughout the Bible, both in the Old Testament and New Testament times, we read accounts of God speaking to His people in various ways, sometimes directly and sometimes indirectly.

He speaks through pictures, He speaks through actions, He speaks through His Word, He speaks through dreams and visions, He speaks through your spirit, He speaks through prayer, He speaks through visions, He speaks through other individuals and He speaks directly to us in that 'still small voice' (1 Kings 19:12).

Often when we hear people refer to God speaking or how one should respond in such an experience, it is not surprising that this whole process would appear to be complicated, yet, it is quite the opposite.

When God speaks, He is quite clear. It is just that sometimes when He speaks, what He says may not be what we were expecting or it may not be the answer that we were waiting for. As a result at times, we either fail to recognize or even deny that it is the voice of God. I can assure you that God does still speak and I want to share with you some of my personal experiences. (Matthew 11:15).

When we are in a relationship with another person, we expect some kind of communication; we speak and we expect a response. When we are in a relationship with God we also have two-way communication. However, sometimes this is forgotten; many times we spend much time talking to God but we fail to allow Him to respond to us; always in a hurry to say 'Amen' and finish. God wants and longs to speak to us but we have to be willing to listen.

In his book, 'God Talks to You', Dr Robert Perkinson shares with us how we can know or recognize that it is God speaking to us.

'These are the tests that will increase our confidence that the communication we receive is from God.

- The voice will acknowledge that Jesus Christ came in the flesh.
- The fruit is love, joy, peace, patience, kindness, goodness, faithfulness, gentleness, and self-control.
- A feeling of love and peace will accompany the message.
- The message will agree with scripture.
- The message will glorify God.
- The message will be pure, peace loving, considerate, submissive, full of mercy and good fruit.
- The message will create a humble love for God.
- The message will create a new feeling of life and hope.
- The message will be true.
- Your spiritual friend will agree with the message.
- The message will not tell you to rush in blindly.'

I say to each reader if God speaks to you and asks you to do something, not only will He prepare you; He will also provide both resources and the personnel if necessary to fulfil the task He has given to you.

So, what are you waiting for? Once you know that God has called you or given you a task to do, just do it. There really is nothing complicated about the voice of God as it may often seem. Remember! When God calls you, He equips you.

Join me, read my testimonies as we journey up the mountain and discover the 'faith-building-blocks' that increased my faith in God and helped me to climb the mountain of life.

GOD WILL PROVIDE

Where we were; another day had dawned and there was no food in the house. My husband had a hard week at work and there were three hungry mouths to feed. Fortunately, I have parents who are always there to help in time of need, but there comes a time in our lives when you just have to trust and know that God will come through for you.

This was a Saturday morning, one by one my children came and asked me 'what are we going to have for dinner today?' I told them to look in the cupboards which they did and they found nothing. Then I told them to look in the refrigerator which they did, and again they found nothing. They came and told me that there was no food in the cupboards or refrigerator. My response to them was, 'Don't worry, God will provide.' It is not that we had no one that we could turn to for help but I felt that there are times when we need to depend on God and this was one of those times. I believe that our lives should be a living testimony to the goodness and faithfulness of God.

About two hours after this conversation with my children, there was a knock at the front door. In walked my brother-in-law with several bags of shopping. This was very unusual, as he had never done this before or since. As I emptied the bags one by one, I declared to my brother-in-law that the Holy Spirit had taken him shopping because as I took each item out of the bag, I realized that the bags contained everything that I would have bought, had I been able to go shopping. I gave God thanks as I reminded the children of the earlier conversation.

I did not realize the impact that this step of faith had on my children. This testimony of God's provision for my family remained with them ever since. Many years later the youth group from our local church were planning to do a play. One of my children suggested the topic of 'God Will Provide' and shared the events of this testimony with the group; the play was then based on this experience.

'And it came to pass after these things, that God did tempt Abraham, and said unto him, Abraham: and he said, Behold, here I am. And he said, Take now thy son, thine only son Isaac, whom thou lovest, and get thee into the land of Moriah; and offer him there for a burnt offering upon one of the mountains which I will tell thee of.

And Abraham rose up early in the morning, and saddled his ass, and took two of his young men with him, and Isaac his son, and clave the wood for the burnt offering, and rose up, and went unto the place of which God had told him. Then on the third day Abraham lifted up his eyes, and saw the place afar off. And Abraham said unto his young men, Abide you here with the ass; and I and the lad will go yonder and worship, and come again to you.

And Abraham took the wood of the burnt offering, and laid it upon Isaac his son; and he took the fire in his hand, and a knife; and they went both of them together. And Isaac spake unto Abraham his father, and said, My father: and he said, Here am I, my son. And he said, Behold the fire and the wood: but where is the lamb for a burnt offering?

And Abraham said, My son, God will provide himself a lamb for a burnt offering: so they went both of them together. And they came to the place which God had told him of; and Abraham built an altar there, and laid the wood in order, and bound Isaac his son, and laid him on the altar upon the wood. And Abraham

6

stretched forth his hand, and took the knife to slay his son. And the angel of the LORD called unto him out of heaven, and said, Abraham, Abraham: and he said, Here am I.

And he said, Lay not thine hand upon the lad, neither do thou any thing unto him: for now I know that thou fearest God, seeing thou hast not withheld thy son, thine only son from me. And Abraham lifted up his eyes, and looked, and behold behind him a ram caught in a thicket by his horns: and Abraham went and took the ram, and offered him up for a burnt offering in the stead of his son. And Abraham called the name of that place Jehovah-Jireh: as it is said to this day, In the mount of the LORD it shall be seen.' (Genesis 22:1-14)

It would have been so easy to just pick up the telephone and let my parents or my siblings know that we had no food but there was no doubt in my mind that God had answered my prayer even before I had spoken it. This experience also serves to remind us that God has not changed; He is the same yesterday, today and forever. The same God who provided for Abraham thousands of years ago, is the same God who still provides for His people today. God truly is Jehovah Jireh, our Great Provider.

My prayer request:

_____

_____

_____

_____

_____

_____

_____

GOD SPEAKS THROUGH HIS WORD

It was the first night of the National Youth Convention; an annual event of the New Testament Church of God and there I was after a challenging meeting relaxing in my hotel room with my room- mate. I had decided that since I had no intention of attending Bible School there was no need for me to attend the Bible School session the next morning, and therefore, no need for me to retire to bed early.

After some time, I opened my Bible and began to read 2 Timothy 1. Suddenly, the words came alive to me and it was as though they were written specifically for me. As I read verse eleven,

'Whereunto I am appointed a preacher, and an apostle, and a teacher to the Gentiles,' (2 Timothy 1:11). I became fearful. At the time when I read these words, I did not like talking to more than one or two people at a time because I had not yet overcome my fears; I always felt that I was being watched, judged and criticized. Yet, here, in this scripture verse, here was God telling me that I would do more than just talk.

As the fear began to rise, I was immediately taken back to verse seven which has since become one of the key verses for my life – 'For God has not given us a spirit of fear, but of power, and of love and of a sound mind.' (2 Timothy 1:7). This is a verse that I had read many times before without any impact. Now, it was as though the words of the text had suddenly come to life. From that night, the fears that I had over the years began to diminish, little by little, as I allowed the fear to be replaced with the power of the Holy Spirit, the love of God and a sound mind.

Yes, the fears do try to come at times because fear is like a weed; it keeps coming back. Just as you would have to apply weed killer in your gardens to kill the weeds that keep coming back, you have to continually apply the Word to our lives to keep the weeds at bay; such as fear, low self-esteem, etc.

On returning home I made a few phone calls about going to Bible College. I could not understand the responses that I was receiving. Incidentally and on reflection, I did understand what was happening; I just did not have enough faith at that time to just follow God's leading without questioning. All the enquiries that I made through individuals who had or were currently attending Bible School directed me to Birmingham Bible Institute which was a multi denominational college.

This made no sense to me because the church I attended had its own college. It could be that I was not fully persuaded, so God sent someone to my house at the end of that first week. This individual was doing a house to house survey which was irrelevant to my current situation – he was asking general household and marketing questions including toiletries and banking.

When he had finished asking his questions he went on to tell me about Birmingham Bible Institute. How strange! After getting over the shock of the change in the conversation, from survey to Bible College, I realized that I could no longer question God concerning His call on my life. He had spoken to me through His Word, through friends and now because of my doubting He spoke to me through a total stranger. This was now sufficient confirmation for me to know that this was the direction that God wanted me to take and so any doubt had now been wiped away.

I often encourage individuals by saying that when God calls you into ministry or gives you a particular task, He also provides all that is necessary to equip you to complete the task. Some weeks after saying yes to God's call on my life, I discovered that He had spoken to a friend (a sister in Christ) to pay all of my school fees even before He had spoken to me to attend.

This experience was a HUGE stepping stone in my faith walk because God had put everything and every person in the right place for me to complete the task that was set even before I heard His call and before I had even asked about the resources. How awesome is our God? He spoke to someone to take care of all my school fees, He opened the way for me to be accepted into college, He withheld the payment of fees for the first two months to enable my faith to grow (the person that God had spoken to pay my fees had not yet informed me) so I had to begin my course by faith and He allowed my work place to grant me a career break to complete these studies.

'Finally, be strong in the Lord and in the strength of His might. Put on the full armour of God, so that you will be able to stand firm against the schemes of the devil. For our struggle is not against flesh and blood, but against the rulers, against the powers, against the world forces of this darkness, against the spiritual forces of wickedness in the heavenly places.

Therefore, take up the full armour of God, so that you will be able to resist in the evil day, and having done everything, to stand firm. Stand firm therefore, having girded your loins with truth, and having put on the breastplate of righteousness, and having shod your feet with the preparation of the gospel of peace;

In addition to all, taking up the shield of faith with which you will be able to extinguish all the flaming arrows of the evil one. And take the helmet of salvation, and the sword of the Spirit, which is the word of God.' (Ephesians 6:10-17).

What is God saying to you?

_____

_____

_____

_____

_____

_____

_____

_____

_____

_____

_____

_____

GOD SPEAKS IN A STILL SMALL VOICE

'And he said, Go forth, and stand upon the mount before the LORD. And behold, the LORD passed by, and a great and strong wind rent the mountains, and brake in pieces the rocks before the LORD; but the LORD was not in the wind: and after the wind an earthquake; but the LORD was not in the earthquake: and after the earthquake a fire; but the LORD was not in the fire: and after the fire a still small voice.

And it was so, when Elijah heard it, that he wrapped his face in his mantle, and went out, and stood in the entering in of the cave. And behold, there came a voice unto him, and said, What doest thou here, Elijah?

And he said, I have been very jealous for the LORD God of hosts: because the children of Israel have forsaken thy covenant, thrown down thine altars, and slain thy prophets with the sword; and I, even I only, am left; and they seek my life, to take it away. And the LORD said unto him, Go, return on thy way to the wilderness of Damascus: and when thou comest, anoint Hazael to be king over Syria: and Jehu the son of Nimshi shalt thou anoint to be king over Israel: and Elisha the son of Shaphat of Abel-meholah shalt thou anoint to be prophet in thy room. And it shall come to pass, that him that escapeth the sword of Hazael shall Jehu slay: and him that escapeth from the sword of Jehu shall Elisha slay. Yet I have left me seven thousand in Israel, all the knees which have not bowed unto Baal, and every mouth which hath not kissed him.' (1 Kings 19:11-18)

This testimony continues from the previous one. As I said earlier, I did not like talking to people because I always assumed that they would criticize what I said or how I would say it or even how I looked, but I decided that I would answer God's call to study His Word but it was on a conditional basis. My conditions were - I was not going to be a teacher, I was not going to be a preacher, I was not going to be an evangelist, I was not going to be a missionary and so the list went on and on. I was so focused on looking at my current abilities that I put a limit on my life without realizing it and without realizing the implications that this might have.

When you put limitations on your life you are limiting what God can do with you. We look at our lives through finite eyes so what we see or recognize as our abilities or lack of abilities hinders our belief of what we can accomplish. However, if we trust God and allow Him to lead and direct us, we will accomplish far more than we ever will without the help of God.

Eighteen months into the course whilst attending a lecture based on the book of Ezekiel, I heard a voice begin to speak into my right ear. I turned around, but all the other students were seated listening to the lecturer. The conditions that I had put to God at the beginning of the course (eighteen months earlier) were repeated back at me by the same voice I heard speaking into my right ear during the lecture.

The voice was very clear. It asked me, 'If you are not going to be a teacher, you are not going to be a preacher, not going to be an evangelist, not going to be a missionary, not going to use what you are learning, what are you doing here?' I knew it was the Lord speaking to me because the only time I had mentioned these constraints on my life was when I was alone in prayer with God.

I thought about this question for only a few short moments and realized that God could not use me unless I was prepared to take the limits off my life so that His will and purpose for my life could be fulfilled. I responded, 'Okay Lord, I will do whatever you want me to do.' At that time, yet again I did not realize the depth of my response or the impact my response would have on the rest of my life. In my response I was telling God that I would do whatever He wanted me to do, I would say whatever He wanted me to say and I would go wherever He wanted me to go.

Had the reality of what I had said sank in at the time, I do not know if I would have had the courage to verbalize such a response but I thank God that He showed me how purposeless my life would have been if I had maintained the limitations that I had placed on it. I now use these encouraging words for you my reader.

If you are prepared and willing to do what God wants you to do, to say what God wants you to say and to go where God wants you to go; be assured that He will not send you alone, neither will He send you powerless. He is with us all the way and He gives us His Holy Spirit to empower us for the service that He has called us to do.

'And ye are witnesses of these things. And behold, I send the promise of my Father upon you: but tarry ye in the city of Jerusalem, until ye be endued with power from on high. And he led them out as far as to Bethany, and he lift up his hands, and blessed them.' (Luke 24:48-50).

Through the authority of Jesus Christ we can say 'yes' to God without putting restrictions on our lives. Once I had lifted the constraints off my life, there has been greater fulfilment, satisfaction and growth: I have the freedom to speak to people that I would never have spoken to, I have the courage to go places that I

14

would never have considered going and I have the ability through the Holy Spirit to do things that I would never have thought possible.

God sees your past, your present and your future state. He sees you in your fulfilled state, accomplishing great things in your life in Him. However, this can only happen when you learn to look beyond your immediate circumstances and do not allow yourself to be limited by what your natural eye can see or your own abilities. I can do all things through Christ who strengthens me. (Philippians 4:13).

Shhh! Listen! When you pray, remember it is a conversation. What is God is saying to you in the quietness?

_____

_____

_____

_____

_____

_____

_____

_____

_____

_____

_____

_____

_____

_____

GOD SPEAKS THROUGH OTHERS

'And it came to pass at that time, when Eli was laid down in his place, and his eyes began to wax dim, that he could not see; and ere the lamp of God went out in the temple of the LORD, where the ark of God was, and Samuel was laid down to sleep that the LORD called Samuel: and he answered, Here am I.

And he ran unto Eli, and said, Here am I; for thou calledst me. And he said, I called not; lie down again. And he went and lay down. And the LORD called yet again, Samuel. And Samuel arose and went to Eli, and said, Here am I; for thou didst call me. And he answered, I called not, my son; lie down again. Now Samuel did not yet know the LORD, neither was the word of the LORD yet revealed unto him.

And the LORD called Samuel again the third time. And he arose and went to Eli, and said, Here am I; for thou didst call me. And Eli perceived that the LORD had called the child. Therefore Eli said unto Samuel, Go, lie down: and it shall be, if he call thee, that thou shalt say, Speak, LORD; for thy servant heareth. So Samuel went and lay down in his place.

And the LORD came, and stood, and called as at other times, Samuel, Samuel. Then Samuel answered, Speak; for thy servant heareth.' (1 Samuel 3:2-10)

After many years of ministering in the church through varied and numerous roles, the time had come for all the skills that I had learned over the years to come together (Not that I knew this at the time).

I had been attending an annual event called Spring Harvest for a number of years; an event where Christians from different denominations gather for a week of worship and relaxation. A time where I experienced many barriers; social, gender and racial being broken down.

During the intermission of one of the services, I decided to visit the resource centre. I knew exactly where I was going, how to get there and what I was going for. I entered the centre, but to this day I cannot recall just how I ended up in the opposite direction, standing in front of a large map of Africa, in a puzzled state of mind, not knowing how I arrived there or why I was looking at this map. I might add, here, that my friend informed me some weeks later that she knew exactly what God was doing but could not reveal it at the time.

Intriguingly, I stood in front of this map for a while; having come to no conclusion as to why or how I came to be there, I continued to make my way to my original destination. The following day, I attended a seminar entitled 'Faith that Goes' and it was as though God was speaking directly to me through the speaker: calling me to missions ministry.

I attended two further seminars throughout the week where, again I was spoken to about Faith That Goes by individuals who did not know me. Initially I found this quite strange as I had never even considered that my ministry would lead me to go abroad. In fact, I was so convinced that I was not going to be a missionary that I missed most of the lectures on missions when I was attending Birmingham Bible Institute. I had not yet learned to look beyond my circumstances or beyond what the natural eye could see.

By the end of the week I knew quite clearly that God was calling me into missions ministry. However, from the little that I knew of missions, taking this step would mean some significant changes to my family, so I had to ensure that I took the right steps. So, I had to do just one more thing.

I asked four people to pray about the direction that God was sending me in but then, I asked God to confirm this call to missions ministry through four different individuals who knew nothing about what God had been saying to me. Within six weeks I had my confirmation from the four individuals, including one who does not normally say very much.

Once this had happened I began to make preparations and enquiries regarding missions ministry. It was only then that I had a rewarding, satisfying feeling of knowing that I was finally fulfilling my purpose.

What is God is saying to you through His servants?

_____

_____

_____

_____

_____

_____

_____

_____

_____

_____

_____

GOD SPEAKS THROUGH DREAMS

'And it shall come to pass afterward, that I will pour out my spirit upon all flesh; and your sons and your daughters shall prophesy, your old men shall dream dreams, your young men shall see visions: And also upon the servants and upon the handmaids in those days will I pour out my spirit.' (Joel 2:28-29)

I had just enjoyed two weeks in Ghana, where I was recuperating from an illness and I was finally able to spend some quality time with my adopted son and his family. A tremendous storm started in the late evening, so it took a while before we could drift into sleep.

I fell into a deep sleep that night and I had a dream. The enemy (the devil – 1 Peter 5:8-9) was not happy that my marriage was still working, he was not happy that my adopted son and his wife were still together nor that the Missions Ministry of Asantoa Foundation that I had started was becoming successful. So, he was getting ready to attack again, but this time he was coming with reinforcements. In my dream, there were several soldiers outside the house fully armed with rifles and several rounds of bullets. In the dream, my daughter-in-law went out to them to try and bribe them into leaving by giving each of the soldiers some money.

After a short while she came back inside and said they would not listen to her. She looked at her husband and then at me and told me that I had to go out to them. As I began to leave the house I was awakened from my sleep by a sudden crash of thunder from the heavens.

19

The next day I called my son, his wife and a colleague who were with me. I shared the details of the dream with them and told them that we have to be watchful because all the plans that the devil had thrown at us to defeat us had not worked and he was coming with reinforcements.

From that day we prayed earnestly for God's protection in our marriages and in our ministry. As the onslaught came from the enemy, starting with a variety of illnesses, followed by serious disruptions that could have broken the marriages, we were ready because God had forewarned us in the dream. Although many of the disruptions that occurred following the dream were very difficult to deal with, we were victorious because of the victory that was won for us on the cross of Calvary. Victory does not come easily neither does it come without a battle. Fight we did; battle we did; win we did. To God be the glory!

What is God is saying to you?

_____

_____

_____

_____

_____

_____

_____

_____

_____

_____

A Little More Oil in my Lamp

'And God is able to make all grace abound towards you; that ye, always having all sufficiency in all things, may abound to every good work:' (2 Corinthians 9:8)

It was another beautiful Mother's Day celebration. I spent a portion of the day with my mother and then with my young children who had saved their dinner money to treat me to a meal at a Chinese restaurant. When we left church in the afternoon, I noticed that there was only sufficient petrol in the car to drive another fifty seven miles but we had several places to go before our meal.

By the time we had driven around, there was less than thirty miles of petrol left in the tank. We had a lovely time together and after our meal we returned home which was about another ten miles. I wanted to go to evening service but knew I had no money and not enough petrol in the car to get there and be able to return back home.

However, I really felt an urge to go on this particular evening. I looked up and asked God to allow me to go to the evening service and I boldly left my home with my daughter knowing that there was not sufficient petrol in the car and that I had no money to buy petrol. There are times when you have to use your wisdom and in a similar situation, I would have stayed at home. However, there are also times when you have to demonstrate faith in your God. This was one of those occasions where I just knew that somehow God was going to respond to my step of faith.

We went to church (another seven and a half miles) and on arrival one of the brethren suddenly handed me an envelope with money. This brought tears to my eyes as I gave God thanks for blessing me through this person.

21

I now had money to buy petrol and the petrol station was only five minutes' drive from church.

At the end of service my daughter and I boarded the car and began our journey home via the petrol station. However, for whatever reason, the petrol station was closed. I looked at my daughter as I tried to work out what to do as it was late and we did not have enough fuel to drive around to look for another petrol station. Then I looked up and said, 'Well Lord, I came out in faith, you have provided me with money and I came to the petrol station to fill up. If I drive around to look for another petrol station I may run out of petrol. So Lord, since I left out in faith and I made every effort to get to a petrol station to fill up, I now have to be wise. I need you to put some petrol in my car to allow me to take home my daughter to Great Barr (another eight and a half miles) and then to the petrol station which is near to my home in Erdington.'

I then switched on the engine and started the journey home. I arrived at my daughter's home and waited for her to enter before setting off for the last part of the journey. As I drove off the low petrol signal lit up in the car. However, when I looked down, the gauge was now indicating that I had another fifty-seven miles worth of petrol in the car.

I immediately pulled over and stopped the car in absolute awe at what had just happened. How is it possible for me to do so much driving and the gauge remain at the same place as it was when I first set out? I realized that God had answered my prayer and put petrol in the car. I was so excited; I immediately parked the car and rang my daughter, my parents and a few other people. I just had to let people know that God still hears and answers prayers. He is not dead, He is not asleep, He is alive. Jesus said in Scripture that if we ask anything of the Father in His name that it would be done, this was not just for the Christians of the New Testament times; it is true for us today. Remember that the Word of God does not change; it is the same yesterday, today and forever.

Give God thanks for your miracle.

_____

_____

_____

_____

_____

_____

_____

_____

_____

_____

_____

_____

GOD'S PROVISION

Having ended my last employment due to several mini strokes, it had been some time since I had worked and I decided it was time to get back to work. I joined an employment agency which my previous employer had advised me of. They were so impressed with me at the interview that they decided to employ me temporarily until I found permanent work.

This meant that I could see the permanent job vacancies before they were advertised to the general public. I worked there continuously for three months. However, on the last day I came to the decision that I could no longer work for an agency because of the uncertainty each day as to whether or not I would be working.

While conversing with God that morning, I said 'today I must go home with a permanent job.' I set out for work at the agency confident that, on this day I was going home with a new job. However, as the minutes and the hours ticked by (tick, tock, tick, tock, still no job!) my confidence began to fade.

I became impatient and at midday I began to pack my bags with the intention of leaving the office to go and visit other agencies to find permanent employment. My confidence had diminished but my determination was still strong. None-the-less, in my doubting state, God still heard my prayer.

As I packed my bags, my supervisor brought a new job vacancy to me and told me to give the company a call. I looked through the job description and realized that I had no knowledge of the job criteria as it was with a freight company. However, I was encouraged to call them anyway. When I called I was asked to attend an interview at one o'clock the same day. This was fortunate since the premises were only five minutes' drive from where I was.

I attended unaware of what God was doing. I answered all the questions honestly and I informed the interviewer that I had no experience in freight forwarding industry and all the documentation that he showed me, I had never seen before. I had no idea how to use the programme software that was used to produce the documentation. The one positive thing that I did say was that I was a willing and fast learner.

I left the interview despondent and convinced that I had been too honest and I had talked myself out of a job. I made my way back to the office to finish packing my things to leave. When I was almost finished, my supervisor came and told me that she had just received a call regarding my interview. The employer wanted to know if I could start at two o'clock in the afternoon, that same day.

God promised in His Word that He would answer even before we ask. He never goes back on His Word.

'And it shall come to pass, that before they call, I will answer; and whiles they are yet speaking, I will hear.' (Isaiah 65:24)

What do you want God to do for you?

_____

_____

_____

_____

_____

_____

_____

What can you do for God?

_____

_____

_____

_____

_____

_____

_____

_____

_____

ON ANGELS WINGS

In 2006 on one of my many visits to Ghana, I and several missionary volunteers were travelling down a long, dusty road from Kumasi to one of the villages in the Western region.

As usual we were talking intermittently, laughing and taking in the scenes of life in Ghana. After travelling for an hour or two we became part of a traffic jam, which was not in any way unusual except that it was an unusually long traffic jam for this road. In the distance, ahead of us a large group of men were gathered.

The driver's mate left the vehicle to investigate the cause of the hold up of traffic. It was reported to us that ahead was a section of road that was built over a small stream or river. Its support structure was unstable and the road was showing signs of collapsing under the pressure of the traffic. As a precaution, vehicles were crossing this section slowly and one at a time. The group of men were there to assist if a vehicle and its passengers were to run into problems on the unstable road.

I do not know how the others travelling with me felt, apart from the initial astonishment of the predicament, but I had a calmness and a peacefulness about me that could have only come from God. I have learnt so much about the peace of God. We all began to pray and as I prayed, I began to ask the Lord to place His angels all around the vehicle to take us safely past this stretch of road.

As we travelled toward this section of weakened, unstable road, I had an amazing experience. It felt as though the angels of the Lord had not only surrounded the vehicle but gently lifted it and carried us across. It really felt as though we had indeed travelled on angels wings (Exodus 23:20). 'Behold, I send an Angel before thee, to keep thee in the way, and to bring thee into the place which I have prepared.'

Hmm! Are you facing a situation that you need God to intervene?

_____

_____

_____

_____

_____

_____

_____

_____

_____

_____

_____

_____

_____

_____

_____

_____

_____

_____

POWER IN THE NAME OF JESUS

Acts 3:1-16

Whilst in Ghana at the end of a relaxing evening out with my adopted son, his family and my colleague, as we made our way back home, my breathing became difficult: I felt as though I was beginning to have an asthma attack. My breathing had been getting progressively worse over the last few days, but this night it was particularly bad.

I used my inhaler as usual, but there seemed to be no change. In fact, despite the medication my breathing just kept getting worse. As the night rolled on I continued to struggle to breathe. Then at about 3.00am my breathing began to ease.

The following morning I was determined to go to church, so I prepared myself and went. I took my time, as I was very tired from the lack of sleep. As I sat in church I could feel my breathing getting worse again, but at the same time I could hear a voice whispering in my ear. With the expression of laughter the voice mocked and laughed at me telling me that I had come to church and I could not even give God praise. For those of you who know me, you know that I absolutely abhor anything to do with the devil. I felt my breathing getting worse so human logic suggested that I should have just sat quietly. However, this voice persisted, so I decided that regardless of how I felt, I was going to let the enemy know that he had lost the battle yet again and so I began to worship God with all my heart even though it took a lot out of me physically.

It was a real battle because as I worshipped I was feeling stronger spiritually but weaker physically. Throughout the rest of the day my breathing continued to be unpredictable and my inhalers were not having the desired effect. At the same time my breathlessness did not feel like an asthma attack because I was not getting the tightening that I would normally have with an asthma attack. I tried to take it easy for the rest of the day, but as the evening came my breathing was progressively deteriorating again and it felt as though my strength was slowly ebbing away.

As the night wore on, my breathing did not improve. At this point you may well ask, why did I not call for an ambulance or why did I not get a taxi and go to the hospital? At that time in the area we were, there was no ambulance service and to get a taxi you had to walk to the main road and just wait, and hope that a taxi would come along. At night this was highly unlikely.

By the following morning I had become so weak that I could not even stand. As I lay on the floor struggling for breath, the devil had the audacity to come and stand before me laughing. He thought that he could fool me into thinking that because I could not shout for Jesus, that I was defeated. I looked him in the face and challenged him. 'How dare you think that you can stand in my face to tell me that because I cannot shout the name of Jesus that He (Jesus) cannot help me.

In my weak state I laughed back at the devil as I began to call the name of Jesus. It was barely a whisper as I was very weak but I continued to call His name. You see, I knew that the power of the name of Jesus was nothing to do with how quietly or how loudly I could call His name, the power is IN the name of Jesus.

I prayed no prayer. I asked nothing of God. I simply said Jesus repeatedly. As I continued to say the name of Jesus, I felt strength seep into my body until I was able to stand without assistance, walk to the bathroom and prepare myself for the day ahead. I still had to go to the hospital but because of the power in the name of Jesus I

30

was able to walk to the taxi that took me to the hospital rather than having to be carried out.

My friend! Be assured, there is power in the name of Jesus. Don't be afraid or ashamed to call His name in whatever situation you face.

Do you know the power that is in the name of Jesus? Did you know that you are authorized to use that power? What are your thoughts?

_____

_____

_____

_____

_____

_____

_____

_____

_____

_____

_____

_____

_____

_____

GOD MOVES IN MYSTERIOUS WAYS

'For my thoughts are not your thoughts, neither are your ways my ways, saith the LORD. For as the heavens are higher than the earth, so are my ways higher than your ways, and my thoughts than your thoughts.' (Isaiah 55:8-9)

This testimony continues from the previous one. On arrival at the hospital, the Doctor could not understand the symptoms that I was having, but then neither did he ask for my medical history. In fact, he appeared to do no investigations at all. Despite this lack of medical history, within a couple of hours, he decided that there was a possibility of five ailments that could be causing my symptoms.

Then, the doctor decided that there was a sixth option; if I was not suffering from any of the five ailments suggested, then I must be pregnant. In my extreme annoyance I chose the safest option of laughing at his suggestion. I had to ask for the boxes of all the medication that he was giving me and then inform him that they were contributing to my deterioration as they had conflicting symptoms and side effects. However, on a serious note, the insurance medical team were horrified as they realized that he was actually pumping me with medication for all five ailments 'just in case' and I was deteriorating very fast. I no longer had the strength to even eat or drink; I just about managed to sip water from a spoon in extremely small doses. If I stayed under his care any longer, you would not be reading this testimony now.

We were quickly flown to one of the main hospitals in Accra, Ghana that same evening where we spent a few days. This time my medical history was taken from me. Unfortunately, as they began to do tests and treat me they acknowledged that they did not have all the equipment needed to help me. Rather than keep me there untreated they informed the insurance company who arranged for my colleague and I to be flown to South Africa.

I have to admit at this point for just a very short while my faith wavered. I knew nothing about South Africa; the only thing that kept springing to my mind was apartheid and even that I did not fully understand. The arrangements were made for our departure that night and the next morning we made ready to leave for South Africa.

Unfortunately I was so weak that I had to be attached to the oxygen and other medical devices. I was transferred from the hospital bed to a stretcher which took me right to the door of the aeroplane. The only time that I was allowed to walk was to climb the steps of the plane we were to board which I did with great difficulty. I was reattached to the machines once I had reached the cabin.

I was put to lie down, but after a while even with the oxygen I was struggling even more to breath so I was transferred to a seat because as I was raised up, my breathing became easier. I felt on occasions, as though I was drifting away from my body but at the same time I felt quite peaceful.

I heard the doctor suddenly shout something like "Quick, her vitals are dropping" followed by a lot of rushing movements from both the doctor and the nurse. I was unaware of what they were actually doing but I do remember trying to say to them "I'm alright; it's just that my breath seems to be going away".

Rather a non-dramatic statement, I know and maybe I should have been concerned considering I felt as though my life was coming to an end. All I felt was God's peace so at that time there was no fear for my life. For a while I did not know what was happening but sometime after, I was again aware of my struggle to breathe.

The aeroplane stopped once to re-fuel and we continued on our journey to South Africa. On arrival we were transferred directly from the plane to an ambulance and were taken to the hospital. I have to say all my fears were immediately laid to rest; we were treated like VIPs. Although I was still a little concerned as I still knew nothing about South Africa or its culture and customs.

I left the task of contacting my family and close friends to George, my adopted son who had remained with us until we had to be flown to South Africa. We arrived at the hospital and after many questions, many tests and what seemed to be a long assessment, we were finally transferred to a ward.

To my amazement on waking after a few hours sleep we were welcomed by the sound of prayer. I was so overwhelmed; although I was away from my family and friends God had put us onto a hospital ward with patients who were a part of the bigger family, the family of God. It was an awesome experience to know that I knew nothing about the country and I knew no one in this country, yet I did not feel like a stranger when I woke up on this ward.

During my time at this hospital in South Africa I had to undergo many tests and scans. My lungs were only working 57% and I was experiencing a lot of pain in my legs. I was very weak and eating had become a major task. However, whilst my colleague and I were being treated, we were ministering to the other patients, to their visitors and even to the staff. I have learnt over time that we should try our best to see what opportunities God is placing in front of us in whatever situation we are faced with, or circumstance we are placed in.

We were able to minister to one patient when her family were unable to be with her through the Word of God (the Bible), prayer and in song as she lay dying. We were also able to minister to her husband as he watched his wife slipping away to be with her Lord.

We ministered to one lady in her late sixties who had never been in hospital before and so was very fearful of the experience. We were able to minister to one visitor who was trying to give up drugs. We were also encouraged in the Word by nursing staff who would give us our medication and at the same time remind us that we serve a God who heals.

At the start of her duty the matron of the hospital would visit all the patients individually and speak a word of encouragement or a word from the Lord. The whole experience was awesome. We returned to England with far more spiritual healing than physical as a result of the ministry that took place in that hospital.

God really does move in mysterious ways to perform His wondrous works. Many of those whom we ministered to expressed their gratitude to God for sending us to minister to them at the right time.

'For my thoughts are not your thoughts, neither are your ways my ways, saith the LORD. For as the heavens are higher than the earth, so are my ways higher than your ways, and my thoughts than your thoughts.' (Isaiah 55:8-9)

What is your experience of the mysteries of God?

_____

_____

_____

GOD'S APPOINTED TIME

Wait on the LORD, and keep his way, and he shall exalt thee to inherit the land: when the wicked are cut off, thou shalt see it. Psalm 37:34

In April of 2008 as I was attending the Edinburgh Academy of Biblical Excellence. I was about to start teaching about the magnitude of our God when I started to experience an excruciating pain in my lower back. The cause was later found to be a slipped disc and unfortunately I was then confined to hospital for 85 days.

The first twenty days of hospital confinement were very difficult as the frustrations of my predicament blurred my spiritual vision. In other words, I was so blinded by my own needs that I could not see the needs of those around me. It was at the end of the third week as I lay on my hospital bed, I looked up to God and asked God what was the purpose of me still being in hospital as I was becoming frustrated with delays in my discharge.

The answer that I received was to read the Word for Today. I turned the pages and had to smile as I read the topic for the day – Have a Rest. So, I decided to rest in God's peace and as I did so I began to see opportunities for ministry. I then realized that I had missed so many opportunities where I could have been sowing a seed instead of complaining about my predicament.

Many doors opened during my hospitalization. I was able to share the Gospel of Jesus Christ and His saving and healing power, with some of the patients. I was able to let other patients, visitors and staff know that what the doctors say and what tests show is not always the final result and that God can turn the results around.

I began to experience again the peace of God in a difficult situation (see testimony God Moves in Mysterious Ways). Even on the days when I was overcome with pain, I laid a towel which has the words of John 3:16 at the end of my bed so that people received the Word even when I could not speak it.

I have often heard sermons preached and songs sung about the peace of God. This was now my time to experience it and it was indeed awesome. Yet again I found myself in physical pain and still testifying to the greatness of our God and to the peace that is truly beyond our understanding.

Whilst confined to the hospital for 85 days and then to one room in my house because of the pain and inability to walk more than a few steps I was finding it very difficult to focus on reading and writing which is what I normally would have been doing; but the time of physical incapacity also allowed me to take time out and spend some quality time with God.

During this time I re-learned the art of listening to God. Do you know that if we are not careful we can become so busy that we talk, talk, and talk to God and leave without taking any time to listen to what He has to say to us? Before we know it we have drifted from the path of His direction for our lives.

So, although physically weakened I was being strengthened immensely. With my crazy faith I began to plan again how to minister. I started by telling God if I remain in the wheel chair I will minister and if He takes me out of the wheel chair I will minister. You see, we have to be willing to work for God in whatever situation we are faced with. I was not prepared to allow pain or physical disability to stop me from fulfilling God's call on my life.

On Friday 24th October 2008, I endured a gruelling twelve hour journey from Birmingham to Edinburgh to our annual church convention, I had to be assisted in and out of our transportation by my husband and another strong individual. It was about an hour into the service of that evening that I began a conversation with God about the need to be independently mobile and wanting a testimony from this journey.

I told God that I did not want to return to the convention the next day in the wheel chair. After a little consideration I was saying to God that I did not want to wait until the next day but I wanted my healing before the end of the day. As I continued to worship God it suddenly dawned on me that I did not have to wait until the next day. So I started to talk to God again and told God that I wanted healing now and I fully believed that I was right to ask at that time.

Shortly afterward whilst listening to the sermon I heard a gentle voice whisper into my ear. 'Get up and walk around the church' initially I was a little fearful as I looked around the church and almost lost my blessing as even though I had asked and I believed God for my healing, my first reaction when instructed to get up and walk was concern that no-one else was standing (maybe a touch of doubt as I briefly pondered the embarrassment I would experience if …) Despite this pause, I eased forward on my chair and began to move my legs and hips in ways that would normally be painful, but it was not.

I eased further forward and repeated the actions but still no pain. I did this for the third time before finally rising to my feet. Looking back, I realize how much easier it is to talk about faith and belief than to actually put it into practise. As I ponder, it occurs to me that often when the reality of a miracle is put before us, doubt rears its ugly head. Anyway, I was able to put the doubts behind me and stood. It is amazing how we ask God to answer our prayers and then when He does we sometimes behave as though we did not actually believe that He would answer. With my first response, I almost lost my opportunity of an answered prayer. Thank God it was only momentarily. I was not as bold as I thought I was: instead of just getting up as the Lord had spoken to me, I decided to test myself. With every movement that I did that resulted in no pain, it was as though I was gaining spiritually strength. I eventually stood up and began to rock on the spot first before finally walking around the room where the service was being held. It was an unstable walk initially but that was soon rectified. I was now standing, looking down at the wheelchair.

Unknown to me there was a young man present who had recently accepted Jesus Christ as his Saviour. However, there was a problem. He did not believe in physical healing. The following day, seeing the wheelchair parked at the side of the convention room, the young man spent the day looking for the individual whom the chair belonged to who had been healed. Not realizing that it was me, he concluded that yet again, it was all a set up.

On the Sunday, after being called to the front along with the wheelchair and three other individuals who had also received physical healing, the young man suddenly recognized me. As a direct result of this event, that young man is now a fully committed Christian and was baptized on the 4th January 2009.

In the Ecclesiastes 3:1-8, we are reminded that within God's infinite wisdom there is a time for everything. In my opinion, I do not think that we really appreciate the importance of time and we want things to happen in our own time. I know that people have been praying for me across the world and of course many would have wanted to be there at the point of my healing.

However, this was not to be. God's appointed time for my healing was so that God and God alone received the glory and so that His purpose could and would be fulfilled. I now minister in a totally different way but more importantly, God's sovereign move affected change in the lives of many so that His Kingdom people can minister more effectively.

I encourage every reader to wait on God's appointed time but whilst waiting, seize every opportunity that God has placed before you to effect change in the lives of those whom you meet. God bless you and keep you as we learn together to let the peace of God reign in our hearts and become alive when in the midst of the storms of life.

What do you need right now?

_____

_____

_____

_____

_____

_____

_____

_____

_____

_____

_____

_____

FINAL WORD

The God that we serve never changes: the same yesterday, today and forever (Hebrews 13:8).

Jesus Christ the same yesterday, and today, and for ever.

I hope this book of testimonies has reminded you that miracles are not a thing of the past, they are not fictitious, but they are very real.

Jesus said that if we ask anything in His name it would be granted to us (John 14:13). Do you believe?

And whatsoever ye shall ask in my name, that will I do, that the Father may be glorified in the Son.

GLOSSARY

Evangelist – one who preaches the Christian Gospel

Holy Spirit - The Third Person of the Christian Trinity or Triune God.

Jesus – the central figure of Christianity

Lord – one of the names used of God or Jesus

Asantoa Foundation – a not-for-profit organization that does voluntary work mainly in Ghana helping those in need.

Brethren – fellow Christian believers

Word of God – the Bible